rhapsody 2017

an anthology of guelph writing

VP

Vocamus Press
Guelph, Ontario

Presented by Friends of Vocamus Press

Published by Vocamus Press

Cover image by KC Hornsby

ISBN 13: 978-1-928171-62-1 (pbk)
ISBN 13: 978-1-928171-61-4 (ebk)

VP

Vocamus Press
130 Dublin Street, North
Guelph, Ontario, Canada
N1H 4N4

www.vocamus.net

2017

Preface

The Rhapsody Anthology is an annual collection of poetry presented by Friends of Vocamus Press, a non-profit community organization that supports literary culture in Guelph, Ontario.

The anthology is a celebration of local writing that includes both authors who are well established in their craft and those who are published here for the first time, reflecting the writers and writing that formed the literary communities of Guelph during the year 2016 / 2017.

The cover art was provided by Daniel Rotsztain. The cover and interior were designed by Jeremy Luke Hill.

Acknowledgements

The *Rhapsody* anthology is produced by Friends of Vocamus Press, a non-profit community organisation that supports writing, publishing, and book culture in the Guelph area.

This season our work has been generously supported by Nick Dinka, Alec Follett, Andrew Goodwin, Jaya James, Sheila Koop, Kim Lang, Jane Litchfield, Bieke Stengos, and Janice Wiseman. We appreciate their support very much. If you'd also like to support the work of Friends of Vocamus Press, you can do so by searching us on www.patreon.com.

Thanks to all the contributors for sharing their work so generously. Special thanks to KC Hornsby for allowing his art to be used for the book cover. Thanks finally to all those who contribute to the literary culture of Guelph as readers, writers, publishers, sponsors, venues, broadcasters, and in countless other ways – this collection is a celebration of all that you do.

rhapsody 2017

an anthology of guelph writing

CONTENTS

Present-Continuous

Zane Koss

Zane Koss is a poet and a co-founder of the &, Collective, a group of Guelph poets exploring collaborative and experimental approaches to poetry. His debut volume of poetry, Warehouse Zone, *was published by Publication Studio Guelph in 2015. He is currently pursuing a PhD through New York University.*

Present-Continuous

[*there is a gap
between the past and
present participle
that can never be
breached*] Extensive   searches
are being conducted in a 25
km radius around her
property, with no luck.
RCMP are saying there is
nothing to indicate foul
play. RCMP are saying
her disappearance is
unusual since her vehicle,
personal belongings,
medication and dogs
are still here. She is living
happily in a shack with
out running water or
electricity. The last
time they are seeing her
is August 29, 2007.

What We Know and Don't Know
Valerie Senyk

Valerie Senyk is a multi-media artist. She received a BFA and an MA in Drama from the University of Saskatchewan, and taught Theatre Arts at universities in Saskatchewan and Ontario. She is a playwright, an actor, and a performance poet. She has also published a full-length volume of poetry, I Want A Poem *(Vocamus Press).*

What We Know and Don't Know

I try to imagine how
my speech sounds to the Chinese ear

I think: slow, serious
vowels shortened
consonants snapped and pushed

Theirs a cacophony
vowels lengthened
tones rise, fall, flatten, dip

To speak Mandarin I need
to reshape my mouth

reshape my heart

the groundhog in my backyard teaches me about decolonization

Amelia Meister

Performing under the stage name "Meme", Amelia Meister has represented Guelph in 2013 at the Canadian Individual Poetry Slam and in 2011 and 2013 at the Canadian Festival of Spoken Word. She has written two poetry chapbooks: New Eyes on Old Messes *and* Intermezzo.

the groundhog in my backyard teaches me about decolonization

he says you are the medicine animal
because this is what you eat:
violets, dandelions, yellow dock

you do not touch the goutweed:
a strange invader with questionable ethics

he says i can make drums from your skin
like the Wyandot, Seneca and Cayuga
they filled the clay pot with water
pulled your hide tightly and
you drank eternally in their ears

he says you're probably pregnant again
this year more medicine animals
more little drums
to eat my peas and beans
to destroy my lettuce and beets

Grassland
(The prairie wolf and the bee)
Anna Bowen

Anna Bowen is a freelance writer and editor based in Guelph, Ontario. She has an MA from the University of Toronto and a diploma in Creative Writing from the Humber School for Writers. Anna Bowen's writing can be found in Alternatives Journal, Geez Magazine, This Magazine, Momentum Magazine, *and* Spacing. *Her new volume of poetry is called* ReMediate.

Grassland (The prairie wolf and the bee)

The brush wolves hear your new name –
grassland
a top-of-the-soil translation
it comes to them over the downs
and turns their heads eastward

A whining call rises,
whoops circle Phragmites' mis-haloed head

The rusty patch bees, listening
imagine thicket swamps
map lines elude them
but they smell the rumour of willows

They read lines in a ridge of tall grass
the pollen of swamps,
dampness of rat burrows

The coyote's paw crushes barn grass near-silently
as it walks, as if on water
in the miracle of not-sinking.

The landfill breathes an audible breath
and across the trickster land
the prairie wolf calls.

a long season
jeffrey reid pettis

jeffrey reid pettis teaches high school in the Upper Grand District School board. He has published in various magazines and anthologies. He listens to loud music loudly.

a long season

it is a long season that trellises
              of uninhabited silk homes
rest outside my dingy windowsill.
they collect dust
through the ghost of winter
                    and i do not tend them.

i imagine eight tired legs,
bringing themselves home
to rest and resume
              lying in wait.
but it is now december,
and gentle snowdrift
              has crystallized
these abandoned whisp –
palaces.

and i know no spider
who would return to the reflection
of a long-renounced home
to risk the so painfully-refracted
vision –
too much amplified
for eight eyes –

of such blinding light
        and fragility.

Love
Greg Rhyno

Greg Rhyno has published a novel To Me You Seem Giant *(NeWest Press). His fiction has appeared in* PRISM International, *and he is a recipient of the J. Alexander Munro Memorial Prize for poetry. Greg has also recorded and toured with such rock n' roll outfits as The Parkas, Phasers On Stun, and Wild Hearses. He works as a high school teacher in Guelph, Ontario.*

Love

I wrote your name in beach sand,
But the tides took it
And scattered you across foreign waters.

In the Atlantic,
The first letter became a lamprey,
And fed off a small population of haddock
Near the British Isles.

The third became a vermiform
Living in the kidney of a bottom dwelling octopus,

While the fourth became a more notorious member
Of the order elasmobranchii,
And devastated tourism and trade in Fort Lauderdale.

But the second letter remained unchanged.
It floated across the Adriatic,
Like a small life preserver,
Around which the others gathered,
To circle beneath my toes.

Ray Romano: Patron Saint of Trivial Comforts

Mike Chaulk

Mike Chaulk is a founding member of &, collective. His work has appeared in PRISM: International, filling station, Matrix, Up Here, *and on the* Lemon Hound *blog. He punched years as the Associate Poetry Editor of* The Incongruous Quarterly *as well as Editor-in-Chief of* The Void Magazine *at Concordia University. His manuscript,* Night Lunch, *was shortlisted for the 2014 Robert Kroetsch Award for Innovative Poetry.*

Ray Romano: Patron Saint of Trivial Comforts

Drove, sure we did, along narrow 37A, the long while
our odds splattering the cliff faces our high-beams
catching snowmelt spitting from cracks, blood from ears,

reflecting off road signs that warned against boulders,
under easy avalanche in the possible night air pressed
from us; warning us, on watch for moose, bears, burial –

   Debra! Raymond whines, taking
       his loafers off before bed,
he and I like two minivans passing in the night –

which, my fears not wholly unfounded. For one, juneo06
onCarGurus.com, regarding the 2001 Kia Sedona,
warned, engine no power weak; for two our fuel gauge,

its ticking how long since the last fill, anyone else seen.
They know better, the Northern May better, its dangers
and glaciers' crawl, chased us, finally, to The Next Nearest

Motel, its thawing child-receptionist humming along
to a broken bulb, pastel-blue paint, the town asleep,
its fuel and families locked up: border workers, many likely

Why does everyone here own a truck?, I ask. You think
they all need one? Like actually need?, the long while Ray
complaining of pillows: a straight middle class white man

to me, a cozied close call on the edge of Alaska grips
tight the old remote, begs Ray not to turn off his lamp.
I need you like a sitcom, Ray. Our pillows, Ray. Us.

She Moves Like a River
Jerry Prager

Jerry Prager is a former community newspaper editor, published poet, improv musician, playwright, historian, chef, canoe trip guide and stone worker, actor, dancer and under-employed jack-of many trades. He has published books of poetry, fiction, and history. Jerry currently resides in Elora.

She Moves Like a River

She moves like a river in the folds of her rhythm,
ripples her murmurs and rides the bed in steady time,
she rolls through rises and eases down slides
she's got deep places where she moves coriolis inside,
she eases her momentum and then lets it slide,
falls tributary to pleasure, follows their currents,
gathers flow, sluices and courses sublime,
stretches primordial, cascades in full spate
erupting, then drifts through flood meadow
makes her way to my mouth;
becomes estuary
in waves and ripples
that shudder and linger
caress skin like shoreline laps
with her tongue
skipping stones of pleasure
one after the other, my turn
before she stills like breathing lakes
awaiting resurgence.

Yellow Cessna

Candace de Taeye

Candace de Taeye's poetry has been published in CV2, Carousel, Echolocation, Feathertale.com, *and* Joypuke. *Her first chapbook,* Roe, *was published by PS Guelph. Her debut full-length collection,* Small Planes and the Dead Fathers of Lovers *is available from Vocamus Press.*

Yellow Cessna

first this old man dapper despite his body
odor, worn mink cap. offered me a flight

small yellow Cessna. we flew over the fields tobacco potato
tombstones of dead pets my childhood home a quarry

the whole town could tessellate into
unbeknownst to me. we start and end low

over the house where my future
father-in-law will die in my arms.

decades ago the man in the mink cap was paid
$50 a piece for each snowy owl he trapped.

Temagami
Paul Hoy

Paul Hoy is a poet residing in Guelph, Ontario. His poetry is shaped by the natural landscape and the wilderness of northern Canada. He admires the poetry of Jim Harrison, Jack Gilbert and Seamus Heaney and the prose of Ernest Hemingway, Richard Ford and Cormac McCarthy. He studied English Literature at the University of Toronto.

Temagami

Naked, we are used to pointing out each other's bruises.
As if anything can be done. We walk slowly, teetering,
our arms suspended, like falling birds, while our feet land,
stinging with pinecone, pinched by whetstone jaws.
We hear wind possessing forests, lakes constantly
shuffling on shores, or that lay content in bowls
they've shaped with Precambrian ash.
We dive, front-crawling as far as we can go.
Underwater, we open our mouths to speak.
Clouds of pop and riffle, each of us sound
the same to the other. We never understand.
You feel my heartbeat when I enter you, deep as I can,
sonar finding boulders weighted down by shadows,
or warmth cloaked in cold. Finding something unbreathable
in you. We've seen fish far out beyond the island boats.
Together, we could swim there. Their green sails seem bright
with hope that shimmering distance washes away bruises.
We do not belong there, but we could go.

I Saw a Sign
Darcy Hiltz

Darcy R. Hiltz grew up in Nova Scotia and moved to Ontario in 2004. A graduate of Acadia and Dalhousie University he holds a Certificate of Creative Writing from Conestoga College. He has published a chapbook of poetry called Beyond All This *(Fenylalanine Publishing, 2015). He currently resides in Fergus Ontario.*

I Saw a Sign

from the road,
"Retreatants Welcome"
on the outskirts of municipal bounds
alongside
a big box battlefield
where the chain of commerce
borders Jesuits
"Retreatants Welcome"
as if calling ghosts
of Wal-Mart Warriors
home

Walking the Corpse Home
James Clarke

James Clarke is the author of almost twenty books of poetry and memoir, including Dreamworks, Forced Passage, How to Bribe a Judge, L'Arche Journal, A Mourner's Kaddish, The Raggedy Parade, Silver Mercies, *and* The Way Everyone is Inside. *He is a former Superior Court judge, and his judgements have been published extensively in legal journals. He lives in Guelph, Ontario.*

Walking the Corpse Home

The old poet, lost within himself, is walking
home backwards as they say in China. He has

assigned himself the hard work of memory,
refuses to die on some dusty road in a foreign

land far away from his hearth. Alert to the
hungry ghosts within him, he rises early to

track the morning sun, revisit old haunts &
hurts, determined to make amends for all the

defections & missteps of the first half of life
when he was too callow & mindless to pay

attention. He is walking backwards to find
himself, living his life twice. He is going home.

To Marjorie 1968
Donna McCaw

Donna McCaw has written two books of poetry: Spiral to the Heart *and* The Spell of Crazy Love. *She has also written a two short story collections:* Sing a Song of Six Packs *and* Under the Apple Boughs. *She organizes Wordfest in April and October at the Elora Centre for the Arts, and does storytelling at various venues.*

To Marjorie 1968

Long frizzy brown hair free of curlers or perms,
Dark thatches sprouting from armpits.
She studied sciences, was pragmatic.
When I asked what she saw in Roger,
"A great body, good genes, energy, enthusiasm."
No projections, no romantic notions.

When her daughter came screaming into her world,
Roger left.
She was neither surprised nor wounded.
She plopped little Asia on her hip,
Then got a PHD in genetics.

MARCH 3 1999

Nicholas Ruddock

Nicholas Ruddock is author of The Parabolist *(Doubleday 2010),* How Loveta Got Her Baby *(Breakwater 2014), and* Night Ambulance *(Breakwater 2016).*

MARCH 3 1999

There's rock and grass and rabbits, that's about it, dead-still most of the time but for the wind and the sound the waves make on the rocks below — a low-pitched rumbling crump that goes on day and night, the big combers rolling in unobstructed for a thousand miles—and here's this storm-bent picket-fence they used to lean against, he and she unsuspecting (why not, they were only eighteen), their bodies still quick and alive and moving place to place or lying back against the hummocks of grass summertime, shoulder to shoulder, talking, doing whatever they did. Now it's over. From their graves they get to listen twenty-four hours a day to the waves coming in non-stop, and it doesn't matter to them if it's as dark as midnight or noon-time, it's all the same. They'd lift their heads to listen if they could. They're buried here as far apart as possible, by their families, by those who had the power to do so, by the older men who piled up worn tires and poured on the kerosene, struck matches, flipped cigarettes to thaw the frozen ground, who then dug straight down beyond the reach of animals, leaning on their shovels, watching the separate black-licorice strands of smoke bend and rise and intertwine and form the one final shroud that should have been theirs all along, on March 3 1999.

Intimate
Kathryn Edgecombe

Kathryn Edgecombe has been able to indulge her love affair with words ever since she quit teaching and moved to the country. She now spends as much time as possible in her writing cabin by the pond. Her work has appeared in several journals and anthologies, and she has published three books of poetry, Not the First Waltz, Midwives to Our Selves, *and* Draw Me to the Flame.

Intimate

I wanted to watch you shave
        but I didn't
It seemed imperative
        to leave the room
To leave the night before and
        the longing
As if it would tangle around our legs
        trip us
And surrender our dreams

I wanted to put your toothbrush
        in my mouth
Pierce the tip of my finger on the blade
        of your razor
Watch the crimson teardrop form
        on the arch of the moon
And put my finger between your parted
        lips

t * This poem won First Prize in the Open Heart 10 contest held by The Ontario Poets' Society.

No Refuge
Michelle McMillan

Michelle McMillan has been a prolific writer all of her life. Now semi-retired from a full life as a Mother, Museologist, Retailer, Designer, and Gardener; she is grateful to have the time to study and practice the craft of writing. Her writing has been published in Rhapsody, Guelph Speaks, TongRen, *and* Vox feminarum. *She has written a privately commissioned biography and is presently working on a family memoir.*

No Refuge

A chimera roams this falling night.
Her vestments trail
in shifting shadows muffled
under a cloak of velvet,
soft as staghorns moulting.

The sheen of raw silk ripples
across wet pavement strewn
with gold filigree and diamonds,
the crimson flesh of roses,
a splash of pooled silver –
Holy sacrament.

I came here for refuge.
Here where it makes no sense to wander,
where watery darkness blears
the familiar shape of things
and present melts into past
with a steady drip.
In this uncertain place
I find him.

He is continental drift that folds rock,
phantom rain never touching earth,
vibration in my empty hands,
rare eclipse of sun and moon,
shadow ringed in light,
a mirage shimmering.

A flash of chrome splashes my gaze.
Red lights soak through the dark wash
of crushed leaves and shattered glass.
No wedding cake.
I am a cry of joy in a matrix of asphalt.

I was never safe here.

Hollow Cost
Burl Levine

A lifelong resident of Guelph, Burl Levine taught English at Conestoga College for 25 years and has offered freelance writing, proofreading, and editing services through his sole proprietorship INKLINGS ® since 1996. He has also written five books.

Hollow Cost

during the Holocaust,
millions of innocent people
suffered from a caustic calamity
in an era when the word *mankind*
became a contradiction in terms

so let us remember
that if we ever forget
this epically evil episode,
then the price of every sacrifice
will always be regarded
merely as a hollow cost
resonating with agnostic indifference
rather than as a hallowed cost
reverberating with rabbinical reverence

Ar***t macht frei
Bieke Stengos

Bieke was born in Belgium, came to Canada as a young woman, and has lived here ever since, with time spent in various countries overseas. She has published a chapbook, Aunt Ida, *and two collections of poetry,* Abandoned by the Muse *and* Transmigrator.

Ar***t macht frei

In gentle, soft-born, measureless light
I captured you: poisoned
corpse, witness
to countless, who did
not labour freely.
I captured you,
witness to your own
odourless demise.

* The opening line is from Walt Whitman's, "When Lilacs Last, in Door-Yard Bloom'd" lines 11 and 12. The poem was written in response to a display at the Verbeke Foundation – http://www.verbekefoundation.com/en/general-info/.

Seize

Jeremy Luke Hill

Jeremy Luke Hill is the publisher at Vocamus Press and the the Managing Director at Friends of Vocamus Press. He has written a collection of poetry, short prose and photography called Island Pieces, *a chapbook of poetry called* These My Streets, *and an ongoing series of poetry broadsheets called* Conversations with Viral Media.

Seize

There is the moment you come home
from the only home you've ever known,

dressed in four months of joy and two
weeks of counting grief down to this –

when you sleep all through your good-byes,

your carseat falling into place
beneath the dome-light's guilty glow,

and I can't help wonder if it's right
for me to seize you in my heart.

Spectrums of Evidence
Don Proctor

Don has self published four books of poetry and visual art, Blather Drive, The Vacuous State of Multiplicity, Give Duty to the Wind, *and* Stapled Bet to Bare. *He works as a Wastewater Treatment Operator for the city of Guelph.*

Spectrums of Evidence

Shadows flickering in procession to the flame
Undisclosed evidence of a dissected night
The might of the conflagration runs to the void
Precariously veers towards atmosphere and employs
Combustion, thermal expansion
Unification of man and nature by absolution
Burning pure the scattered sins
Hope spurs, raising the ignition of desire
Renders passage from the depth of fire
The inferno burns lucid
That breaks speed to stillness and expands
to a thermal shadow's demands
Cross trekking the bricks
The senses fierce and fluid
The black shadow bellows:
"Climb clean spent, clear vacant light ascend!
Bring me up in stillness freed
that's blacked out inside of me!"
The flick of a flint, shadows diversify the night
Positive and negative space in a nocturnal fight
Vicariously living unto the spectrum of the blaze
Hues spacial to neglected transparency
Worriless, wayward rolling
Eyes of the night
Burn clean and black in unison

Ode to Brazil

Nina Kirkegaard

Hailing from Quebec City, Nina has recently moved to Guelph and discovered her affinity for poetry. Lately, she is writing poems in French and occasionally Spanish.

Ode to Brazil

Frigid Sunday sweetened by bossa nova
A Brazilian blanket drapes my body
Off to Rio
My lack of vitamin D forgotten
Barefoot – samba, fútbol, sand
From Ipanema to the favelas
Fifa consumed
Ronaldinho is my Pelé
Emotions heavy in Brazil
tears and laughter weigh more
The needle reaches the end
Bossa nova no longer
Mom calls to the table
Feijoada awaits
Sweetest treat for minus twenty.

Renovations
Nikki Everts

*Nikki Everts-Hammond grew up in California, immigrated
to Montreal and spent the last twenty-two years in Guelph.
Writing kept her sane along a circuitous career and life
path. She has recently published a chapbook of her poems,*
Connect Dis Connect, *under the auspices of her company,
Scripted Images.*

Renovations

To make new again
It seems unfair
That my bathroom can be renovated
But I cannot

No delving into my inner body
To redo my leaky plumbing
Or replace a moldering part
Of my sagging structural walls

No layering over my flabby flesh
Flaking and fusty from long use
With a smooth new exterior
Sleek, Svelte, Sexy

Dreams

Jessie Winokur

Jessie Winokur is a 28 year old white settler lady living in Attawandaron territory (Guelph, Ontario). She is a poly-math and freelancer with a weirdly specific science degree and a love of poetry, music, and magic.

Dreams

In the beginning
our nightmares tell us we aren't made of stars
the dissonance shakes our bones
when we learn the arrangement of our atoms
tore us
from our raw materials.

Some day we begin to weep in tandem
pin little daisies to our breast
and try too hard to smell and taste
what's missing from our bodies

At last
we stop drawing boxes around our branches
stop measuring what separates
our roots from the soil
hover around tornadoes until
they tire of their own whirling
and die.

missedunderstandings
L. Nesbitt

Editor and writer, actor and playwright, Lauren Nesbitt-Baggerman hails from Alberta, Canada, and has travelled around the world. Finally coming to rest in southern Ontario, she decided to call Guelph home. A member of Crime Writers of Canada, she has just published the first in a series of murder mysteries. She is also a published poet.

missedunderstandings

It was an accident; he looked so embarrassed –
    apologetic

He didn't mean it –

When Gertrude drank from the cup intended
    for her son.

All families have their little misunderstandings

when you're at their disposal.

American Naturalist #1
Madhur Anand

Madhur Anand is a Full Professor in the School of Environmental Sciences and University Research Chair in Sustainability Science at the University of Guelph. She has authored/co-authored over seventy-five peer-reviewed scientific papers and one academic book, Climate Change Biology. *Madhur is also a poet and has co-edited* Regreen: New Canadian Ecological Poetry. *Her first collection of poetry,* A New Index for Predicting Catastrophes, *was published by McClelland & Stewart in 2015.*

American Naturalist #1

The American Naturalist sent me a note
in cursive. He said go to Century Wood Products
where the roads devolve from concrete into gravel, to
"Thirteenth Line". He said the American elm survived
the first apocalypse. So much left we could sample
from stained or unstained shades. So much barn we could rejoice
at the sight of American crows perched on a pole,
a once northeastern tree, afield, anonymous, cold.
And praise the industrial cows, the industrial
grain, and the decrepit barns made of endangered elm.
Fourteen hundred dollars' worth I ordered, and he said
no worries and added the goods and services tax,
his signature economical as a live edge.

The American Naturalist wanted a reply.
Welcome to the Editorial Manager. Please
log in. Please select as many classifications
as you feel covers your interests. But I was on
the way to Marsville, to a rotated red bird's eye
on an electronic map. Through the window I saw

a farm where reproduction rose, a black jagged line
towards the ordinate. Towards day butter futures.
Cash-settled butter. Electronic wheat calendar
swap. Composite hard red winter wheat. Live cattle side
by side. Nonfat dry milk. International soybean.
I threw an apple core into the stock exchange, the
native material of the land, the dirt below.

Browning. No complete death. The same letter expressed in
the gut. In triplicate. From the Himalayas to North
American towns, unfortunately a lifestyle:
a four-year old daughter, double-headed razor blades
coated with gold, a mortar and pestle, sexual
incompatibility, red/black/green colour scheme,
volcano plots, their endemic bodies, the sealing
wax which opens a door, a strategy in the field,
an elm library constructed from pandemic elm.
Dwell time: Oakville, Mississauga, more false positives.
Subtractive, upregulated, inoculated.
Collectively referred to here as New Harmony.
Marked with an asterisk means noteworthy* and forests.

t * The last stanza is a found poem from the cut-up text of Sherif,
S. M. et al. Simultaneous induction of jasmonic acid and disease-
responsive genes signifies tolerance of American elm to Dutch elm
disease. Sci. Rep. 6, 21934; doi: 10.1038/srep21934 (2016).
* "American Naturalist #1" was previously published in Hamilton
Arts & Letters (2016/2017): 9.2.

Ode to a Shirt
Rob O'Flanagan

Rob O'Flanagan has been a newspaper reporter, photo-journalist and columnist for nearly twenty years. He is the author of The Stories We Tell *and* The Blown Kiss Collection, *two volumes of short fiction that began as a CBC Radio series in northern Ontario. His collection of poetry,* Open Up the Sky: A Poetic Conversation, *co-authored with Heather Cardin, is available from Vocamus Press. He lives in Guelph and is currently writing a novel.*

Ode to a Shirt

You will come back around,
I said to the shirt in the closet.

You will come back.

And when you do,
I will part the sea
of oversized suits
and fill you up with
my form once more,
if you are still able
to hold me.

Oracular
Michael Kleiza

Michael Kleiz 's poems have been published in various anthologies and magazines. His poem "Remembrance Song" was chosen as a finalist for the William Collins Canadian Poetry Prize presented by Descant magazine. He is an alumnus of the Wired Writing program at the Banff Centre for Creativity in Alberta. His debut collection of poetry, A Poet on the Moon, *was published by Vocamus Press in 2015.*

Oracular

I

That night when the fire
swirled over our heads
"a madness" you called it
to witness alighting tongue
and testament
to a fired heart.

And you saw us
in our embers not passing
not touching but not strangers
not enemies but not nothing.

II

In fallen leaves,
discovered this day
a starling's remains: wings
feathered and iridescent,

maggots roiled
in their purpose
under the pale sky.

This is the wheel chaining us
to its task,
its periodicity
in step with the cycling moon
and setting sun. All
that we have ever done, gone
in that final turn.

Friends of Vocamus Press

Friends of Vocamus Press is a non-profit community organisation that supports book culture in Guelph and the surrounding area. It runs workshops, writing groups, and writer hang-outs. It offers resources for writers looking to publish their work both traditionally and independently. It promotes readings, launches, and other literary events in the community. It also produces the annual *Rhapsody* anthology. For more information, email info@vocamus.net.

www.ingramcontent.com/pod-product-compliance
Lightning Source LLC
Chambersburg PA
CBHW032030040426
42448CB00006B/796